The Little
of Building Vocabulary

by Keri Finlayson
Illustrations by Marion Lindsay

LITTLE BOOKS WITH BIG IDEAS

Featherstone Education
An imprint of Bloomsbury Publishing Plc

50 Bedford Square
London
WC1B 3DP
UK

1385 Broadway
New York
NY 10018
USA

www.bloomsbury.com

First published 2015

British Library Cataloguing-in-Publication Data
A catalogue record for this book is available from the British Library.

ISBN:
PB 978-1-4729-1855-0
ePDF 978-1-4729-1856-7

1 3 5 7 9 10 8 6 4 2

Printed and bound in India by Replika Press Pvt. Ltd.

This book is produced using paper that is made from wood grown in managed, sustainable forests. It is natural, renewable and recyclable. The logging and manufacturing processes conform to the environmental regulations of the country of origin.

**To view more of our titles please visit
www.bloomsbury.com**

Contents

Introduction   4

Words about our world

Family names   7
Toy talk   9
Going visiting   11
My pet – which pet?   13
At the zoo: who?   15
On the farm   17
My bedroom   19
In the kitchen   21
My perfect house   23

Words about us

What makes me happy!   25
Down in the dumps   27
What interests me?   29
Favourite food   31
I love to wear....   33
This is me   35
Dressing up: people at work   37
Party clothes   39

Words about appearance and texture

Dark and light   41
The rainbow   43
The rough and the smooth   45
Words for 'big'   47
Words for 'small'   49
Size similes   51
Near and far   53
Shapes   55

Words about movement

Need for speed   57
Steady as a snail   59

Speed similes   61
Moving on up: making a mountain   63
Moving down low: wiggly worms   65
Twirling and whirling: spinning tops   67
Crouching, kneeling and bending   69
Slipping and sliding   71

Words about sound

The noisy dinosaur   73
In the whispering grass   75
Why does the duck say 'quack'?   77
Words for speaking   79
Vehicles   81
Kitchen orchestra   83
Sloshing and washing   85

Introduction

Vocabulary is the knowledge of words and their meaning. Access to a wide, varied and rich vocabulary enables children to communicate ideas, express feelings and needs, and make meaningful connections with adults and peers. By the age of eighteen months the average child has a spoken vocabulary of around fifty words, with the ability to comprehend a further two or three times more. By exploring and acquiring new vocabulary, children learn that words not only have a function but that they are fun to use.

Putting words to work

Children learn language in a social context. A young child doesn't acquire new vocabulary by just memorising daily lists of words. Words are acquired by hearing and seeing them in action; as language at work.

Vocabulary is developed in a number of ways. In conversations, both observed and as a participatory dialogue, words are understood in context within sentences and heard within social situations. Reading allows children to gain experience of words in context, and for children reading often comes with the aid of visual references. Visual references, or props, are also used in physical real-life contexts: children match vocabulary to objects that are familiar to them. Finally, children learn new vocabulary from explicit language instruction. For words to become working vocabulary, they should be used in a way that enables the young child to express themselves clearly and with confidence.

So how do we put words to work in an early years setting? The answer, as always, lies in the multi-faceted role of the practitioner.

Using songs and rhymes

A child's world is full of unexpected vocabulary, and rhymes and songs can be a rich source of new and unusual words. There are 'tuffets' to be sat on and cradles to rock, and many intriguing words can slip into a child's vocabulary almost unnoticed. An enthusiastic practitioner should explore these words, giving the child the ability to apply them in new contexts, enriching their vocabulary as a result.

Providing spaces for vocabulary to flourish

Creating an environment that encourages children to communicate with each other and with the adults who look after them is not always easy in an early years setting, where there are many demands requiring a practitioner's attention. Children often raise their voices to be heard or rely on physical cues to communicate needs, and answers from adults are sometimes unintentionally rushed because of the necessity of an immediate response.

The Tickell Review (2011) suggests that:

Children need a natural flow of affectionate, stimulating talk, to describe what is happening around them, to describe things that they can see, and to think about other people. This is critical for children's language and cognition, their general capacity to engage with new people and new situations, and their ability to learn new skills.

By creating a vocabulary-rich environment in which word sounds are readily heard, children will learn that words can convey instructions, describe the physical world around them, and can enable them to describe their own thoughts, feelings, needs and wants.

The practitioner's use of vocabulary

In an Early Years setting it is the practitioner who sets the language standard. Whether we are giving opportunities for dialogue between pairs or groups of children or explicitly teaching new words, we are always modeling language and the way it is used.

All activities in this book require adult participation. Adults should model key vocabulary in dialogue with children, whether the activity involves moving soft toys up a mountain of cushions or splashing and pouring in a water tray. Vocabulary is widened through repeated use in a variety of contexts.

▶ Always include a vocabulary discussion when preparing for an activity.

▶ Make a note of any unusual vocabulary that might arise; explore and reinforce the words through repeated use.

▶ Relish and enjoy the sounds of new words; pronounce clearly and carefully.

Understanding the gaps

It is often the case that children appear to understand a wide vocabulary. In reality, they may be very uncertain of a particular meaning: the meaning is unstable and is not yet fixed, and the children are using other means to make sense of the word and surrounding context. It's important that as practitioners we never assume that a child knows what a word means, as they may have inferred a slightly or even completely incorrect meaning. Again, using vocabulary repeatedly in context will give children a deeper understanding of a word's possible uses.

Vocabulary and the EYFS

The EYFS Development Matters guidance suggests that practitioners:

▶ Use vocabulary focused on objects and people that are of particular importance to children.

▶ Build up vocabulary that reflects the breadth of children's experiences.

▶ Use and encourage talk by pretending that objects stand for something else in play, e.g. 'This box is my castle.'

▶ Add words to what children say, e.g. the child says 'Brush dolly hair', and the practitioner says 'Yes, Lucy is brushing her dolly's hair.'

▶ Talk with children to make links between their body language and words, e.g. 'Your face does look cross. Has something upset you?'

▶ Introduce new words in the context of play and activities.

▶ Use a lot of statements and fewer questions. When you do ask a question, use an open question with many possible answers.

▶ Show interest in the words children use to communicate and describe their experiences.

▶ Help children expand on what they say, introducing and reinforcing the use of more complex sentences.

▶ For children whose home language is other than English, provide opportunities for them to use that language.

▶ Help children to build their vocabulary by extending their range of experiences.

▶ Foster children's enjoyment of spoken and written language by providing interesting and stimulating play opportunities.

▶ Extend vocabulary, especially by grouping and naming, exploring the meaning and sounds of new words.

▶ Use language to imagine and recreate roles and experiences in play situations.

▶ Ensure that all staff regularly model the use of key vocabulary.

Family names

We have lots of words to describe our different family members, and these vary widely across regions and cultures. By exploring the different terms people use to describe their relatives, children not only gain access to new vocabulary – they can also gain an all-important understanding of cultural difference.

What you need:

- ▶ Large sheets of sugar paper
- ▶ Crayons
- ▶ White card and scissors
- ▶ Low washing line and pegs
- ▶ Wooden lollipop sticks
- ▶ PVA glue

Preparation:

▶ Draw four large windows and a door on the sheet of sugar paper. Cut out the windows, and cut along three sides of the door and fold it so it opens.

▶ Peg the paper house on a washing line suspended at child height.

▶ Cut out circles of white card, enough for more than one per child.

What you do:

1. Discuss the people who are our relatives. What names do we have for these relationships? Do not discuss individuals' names, just the relational terms.

2. Offer the children circles of white card, and ask them to draw the face of someone in their family on one of these cardboard circles. They may draw as many faces as they have relatives!

3. Ask the children to fix the faces to the wooden lollipop sticks using PVA glue.

4. Encourage the children to pop the lollipop relatives in and out of the washing-line house!

Key words:

Family	mum	dad	step-dad	nephew
step-mum	brother	sister	cousin	niece
grandma	grandad	aunt	uncle	step-brother
step-sister	half-brother	half-sister		

Further fun:

There are lots of different words for family members. Look at the different words for 'Mum' and 'Grandma', for instance:

Mum	Mummy	Ma	Mother	Mam	Mata
Grandma	Nana	Nanny	Granny	Mamgu	Bibi	Nani

The various words we have for these different family relationships are a useful starting point for discussion. Ask the children:

▶ Do you use different words for the same person, at different times?

▶ Do your friends use any different words for their relatives?

Toy talk

The topic of toys is a familiar one to young children. Toys are given, requested, desired, shared and judged. Use the importance of toys to encourage children to articulate their feelings and observations, and to develop their social interaction skills.

What you need:

- ▶ Real world objects
- ▶ Soft toys
- ▶ Dolls
- ▶ Construction toys

Preparation:

▶ Ask the children to sit together on the carpet.

▶ Lay out your selection of real world objects and toys, carefully naming and describing each toy as you do so.

What you do:

1. Ask each child to chose a toy (or object) that they like to play with.

2. Ask the child to name the toy and respond to the following questions:

   ▷ What game do you like to play with the toy?

   ▷ Can you describe the toy to us? What colour is it? Is it more than one colour?

   ▷ What does the toy feel like?

3. As the child answers each question, repeat key vocabulary and ask the child to expand on their answer.

Key words:

| red | green | blue | soft | hard | round | square |

Further fun:

The various words we have for these different toys are a useful starting point for discussion.

▶ Ask the children to give a 'speech' about their favourite toy, and model being an appreciative audience. More reticent children can give the 'speech' to you one-to-one later, once the children are playing with the toys.

▶ Encourage the children to continue using appropriate vocabulary as they play.

Going visiting

Sociable mealtimes should be regular occurrences in a child's life, and they provide important opportunities for children to learn new vocabulary and become more confident speakers. This activity helps children to develop their social skills and peer interaction, as well as offering an opportunity for them to learn some fun and useful new words.

What you need:

▶ Home area/ role play area
▶ Food and drink related play equipment

Preparation:

▶ Set up a 'house' area in your role play area.

▶ Ensure that an assortment of food and drink play equipment is available.

What you do:

1. Discuss the word 'visit':

▶ Who might we visit?

▶ Why might we visit them?

▶ What often happens when we visit someone?

▶ Model key vocabulary to the children.

2. After the discussion, introduce the children to the house in the role play area and encourage them to explore different 'visiting' scenarios using the resources available and their imaginations! Encourage the use of key vocabulary.

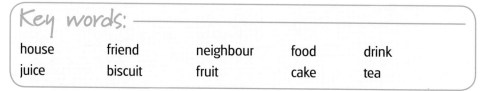

Key words:				
house	friend	neighbour	food	drink
juice	biscuit	fruit	cake	tea

Further fun:

▶ Discuss and name the varieties of food and drink that might be offered when visiting.

▶ Practice pronouncing interesting food vocabulary. Can the children think of any alternative words for 'food', for instance? Can they think of any other new words to do with food and drink?

My pet — which pet?

Even if children don't have a pet at home it's likely that they know someone who does, or perhaps you have a class pet. Naming breeds and species of animals provides us with some very exciting word sounds; children often love to describe their pets' attributes in great detail!

What you need:

- Pictures of pets, e.g:
  - cat
  - dog
  - hamster
  - rabbit
  - iguana
  - bird,
  - stick insect
- A laminator (optional)
- A shoebox

Preparation:

▶ Cut out the pictures of pets.

▶ Laminate the pictures if possible.

▶ Place the pictures in a shoe box.

What you do:

1. Discuss the different types of pets that people have and encourage the children to describe their various features.

2. Ask a child to 'pick a pet' from the 'pet box' and tell them not to show anyone else the picture they have picked.

3. Ask the child to describe the pet by using vocabulary related to its features. Remind them that they should not say what the pet is!

4. Ask the other children to try to guess which pet the first child is describing. The person who guesses correctly takes the next turn at picking a pet!

Key words:

fur	hair	feet	tail	whiskers
curly	thick	bushy	wiry	scaly

Further fun:

Ask the children:

▶ Can you bring in a photograph of a pet that you or someone you know has at home?

▶ Can you talk about this pet to the other children?

▶ Can you describe an imaginary pet? Would it have scales and wings? Might it have fur and feathers?

▶ Can you draw your (real or imaginary) pet?

At the zoo: who?

To teach children initial letter sounds, early nineteenth century alphabet primers often contained a range of animals, from eagles and lions to tigers and elephants. Despite the fact that many children may have not visited a zoo, exotic animals remain a key feature of early years literature. These animals provide us with some mysterious and unusual sounding words with which to describe them!

What you need:

▶ Large sheets of card

▶ Scissors

▶ Fake fur fabric: tiger print, leopard print, brown, (for the bear), gold (for the lion), slinky green (for the snake)

▶ A pillow case

Preparation:

▶ On separate sheets of card, draw an outline of a:

▷ tiger

▷ leopard

▷ bear

▷ lion

▷ snake

What you do:

1. Cut the fabric into palm-sized scraps.

2. Place the fabric scraps in the pillow case.

3. Ask the children to take it in turns to pull a piece of fabric out of the pillow case, and to describe the features of the fabric.

4. Which animal might it belong to? Ask the children to place each fabric scrap on the matching animal.

> Key words:
>
> | | | | | |
> |---|---|---|---|---|
> | stripy | spotty | golden | sleek | slinky |
> | smooth | rough | furry | fluffy | |

Further fun:

▶ Take the children on a visit to a local zoo or animal sanctuary. How many interesting words can they find to describe the animals?

On the farm

A visit to a local farm offers a great opportunity to learn new words. If a farm visit isn't possible, however, then this activity uses small world farm sets or soft toys, and farm-themed stories which provide a rich source of vocabulary.

What you need:

▶ A small world farm set

▶ Farmyard animal soft toys (optional)

▶ Farmyard storybooks or videos

Preparation:

▶ Discuss what life is like on a farm.

▶ Watch a short video or read a story as a starter activity, then use the content as a springboard for discussion.

▶ Talk about the routine of a farmer's day. What sorts of jobs do they have to do? What order might they do them in?

What you do:

1. Using the farm set as a prop, ask the children to tell a story of about a morning on the farm.

2. Listen carefully to the spoken narrative and offer key words to the children as prompts.

3. Encourage a collaborative narrative between children.

4. Explore new words as they arise, for example, words such as 'trough' and 'pen'. ('Pen' can be a light-touch introduction to the concept of homonyms.)

5. Use a whiteboard to introduce and explore visual vocabulary.

Key words:

cow	pig	horse	sheep	chicken	feed
hay	straw	tractor	field	water	
trough	pen	fence	shed	barn	

Further fun:

▶ Encourage the children to involve themselves in role-play about farms and farmers by offering a farm-based role-play area. Can you make pens for your animals? Who lives where?

My bedroom

For children, bedrooms are spaces for imaginative play and hours of make-believe. Our bedrooms are also the places where we keep things that are special to us. Talking about their bedrooms provides children with an excellent language-learning opportunity.

What you need:

▶ Offcuts of wallpaper, A4-sized or larger

▶ Scissors

▶ A4 card and glue

▶ A variety of magazine photographs of bedroom furniture and bedding

Preparation:

▶ Cut the wallpaper into A4-sized pieces and stick each piece onto a sheet of A4 card.

▶ Cut out the pictures of bedroom furnishings.

What you do:

1. Discuss what we might have in our bedrooms. What furniture do you usually find in a bedroom? Do the children keep any books or toys in their bedrooms?

2. Look at the magazine pictures with the children and discuss the names of the various furnishings.

3. Discuss the different colours and textures of the furnishings.

4. Encourage the children to choose a wallpaper swatch each. They should then pick two or three photographs of furniture and furnishings that they would like to put in their 'bedroom'. Talk with the children about their choices. What words would they use to describe each item?

5. Support the children in gluing the photographs onto their wallpapered piece of card to create a 2D bedroom.

Key words:

bed	duvet	pillow	pillow case	blanket
pyjamas	lamp	lampshade	wardrobe	chest of drawers
fluffy	soft	squishy	comfortable	

Further fun:

▶ Suggest that the children role-play going to bed/getting up. What might we do before we go to bed and what might we do when we get up? What objects do we use?

▶ How might we feel when we go to bed? Might we feel a different emotion when we get up in the morning?

In the kitchen

A kitchen provides us with plenty of interesting vocabulary: cakes are baked, kettles are boiled and eggs are whisked. With so much going on we can find lots to talk about and so many new words to use. This kitchen activity encourages children to use action vocabulary and to explore new food words.

What you need:

- ▶ Wooden spoon
- ▶ Spatula
- ▶ Whisk
- ▶ Sieve
- ▶ Jug
- ▶ Bowl
- ▶ A4 recipe cards with printed picture instructions (see 'Preparation')

Preparation:

Make recipe cards (one per child or per pair) using the following series of images as numbered picture instructions:

1   A jug and bowl

2   A sieve

3   A spoon

4   A whisk

5   A spatula

▶   Discuss the childrens favourite foods with them.

▶   Focus on and repeat the names of foods that may be new to some children.

▶   Discuss words that might describe appearance, taste and texture.

▶   Explore the cookery equipment together, discussing what you might use each item for.

What you do:

1.   Offer the children the cookery equipment to explore.

2.   Give them the recipe cards and ask them to follow the action instructions.

3.   Leave the recipe itself open ended. What might they be making? A cake? Buns? Scrambled eggs? Let them use their imaginations.

Key words:

whisk	sieve	saucepan	mixing bowl	jug
pour	stir	sprinkle	drop	beat
mix	spread	salty	sweet	crumbly
wobbly	crunchy			

Further fun:

▶   Ask parents and carers to involve children in the preparation of a meal at home.

▷   Can the children help with pouring, spreading, sprinkling and mixing?

▷   Back in the setting, ask the children to share their experience with their friends.

▷   What other special words can they use to describe their cooking actions?

My perfect house

The house of our dreams may contain anything, from a swimming pool filled with jelly to a giant slide instead of stairs. Encourage the children to use their imaginations to talk about what their dream house would be like. Do they need new words to describe their perfect palace?

What you need:

▶ Large sheets of sugar paper

▶ Crayons or felt tip pens

▶ Whiteboard

Preparation:

▶ Ask the children to discuss their perfect house.

▶ What would it have in each room?

▶ Would it have a garden? If so, what would the garden be like?

What you do:

1. Give each child a sheet of sugar paper and access to mark making materials, and ask them to draw their perfect house, including all the fun features they can think of.

2. Come together as a group and ask each child to share their ideas for their perfect home.

3. Write any interesting vocabulary that crops up on the whiteboard or a large sheet of sugar paper, and explore the meaning and use of each word with the children.

Key words:

Collect key words during your discussion, then explore their meaning and repeat and reinforce vocabulary as an activity plenary.

Further fun:

▶ Provide pictures from catalogues for children to create their dream house.

▶ Challenge the children to make their dream house from building blocks, art and craft resources, and small world toys.

▶ Create a 'junk material' home. Use old tubes, pots and cardboard to make a fun-filled, environmentally-friendly model home.

What makes me happy!

The ability to articulate our emotions is a vital skill, and feeling confident enough to express our likes and preferences is very important. This activity encourages children to talk about things that are special to them and helps them to develop a sense of identity.

What you need:

▶ Yellow and orange collage material
▶ PVA glue
▶ Felt tip pens
▶ A4 paper

Preparation:

▶ Draw a semi-circle on each of the A4 sheets to represent a rising sun. Draw five sun rays coming out from the edge of each semi-circle.

▶ Tear the collage material into small pieces.

What you do:

1. Discuss what makes us happy and explore the key vocabulary.

2. Model what might make you feel a certain way, e.g. 'cosy' or 'giggly'.

3. Explain the nuanced difference between 'cheerful' and 'delighted'. In what context would you use these words?

4. Offer the children the collage material and ask them to paste it on their sun outline using PVA glue.

5. Cover the collage with PVA glue so that it dries hard and shiny.

6. When dry, ask the children to use felt tip pens to draw pictures of things or people that make them feel happy onto their sun.

Key words:

giggle	laugh	cosy	contented	cheerful
delighted	smile			

Further fun:

▶ Sing some happy songs! These might include:

▷ 'I'm H. A. P. P. Y'

▷ 'The sun has got his hat on'

▷ 'If you're happy and you know it'

Down in the dumps

We all feel a bit down in the dumps sometimes, but it's important that children are able to express what it is that is making them feel grumpy or sad. By helping children to articulate their frustration, adults can help to solve problems, deal with issues and assist children in moving on from unpleasant feelings. This discussion activity helps children to see the consequences of certain actions or behaviours and helps them develop empathy and understanding.

What you need:

▶ Blank flashcards

▶ A pen

Preparation:

The flashcards act as practitioner prompts. Write out a number of scenarios to use as springboards for discussion. Use the following scenarios as starting points:

▶ A toy you like gets broken.

▶ Someone won't share a toy with you.

▶ You don't want to share a toy with someone else.

What you do:

Show the flash cards one by one and ask the group to discuss each scenario in turn.

1. Discuss how a person might feel in each situation.

2. Encourage the children to reflect on how they might behave in that situation.

3. Ask: 'If we were watching the scene on television, how do you think the person would act? What would their face look like? How would they move their body?'

> Key words:
>
> cross   grumpy   angry   miserable   sad
> disappointed   annoyed

Further fun:

▶ Choose books for story time that address negative emotions. Make sure you make time for further discussion.

What interests me?

Young children have the ability to learn and retain some complex vocabulary if it stems from a particular hobby or interest. Very young children often surprise us by exhibiting a wealth of knowledge about dinosaurs, complex trading card rules, varieties of vehicles or words related to the lives of fictional characters. This simple activity allows children to share their passion with others using topic-specific vocabulary.

What you need:

▶ Objects or photographs related to children's current interests

Preparation:

▶ Bring in objects or photographs relating to your own hobby or interest.

What you do:

1. In small groups, ask each child to share their interest or passion. They should explain what it is and what they like about it.

2. Encourage the other children to ask relevant questions.

3. Make a note of any interesting vocabulary that the children use. Focus on and repeat topic-specific vocabulary.

4. Discuss your own hobby or interest with the children. Bring in photographs, or objects relating to it and show your enthusiasm for it! If you are a crafter, talk about particular tools, techniques and equipment that you use. If you have an outdoor or exercise-based hobby, why not bring in some of your kit or pictures of where you carry out your interest. Focus on sharing interesting words that are related to your hobby.

Key words:

Words related to the children's specific interests.

Further fun:

▶ Have a 'hobby day' in which children show and share their interests.

▶ Ask other members of staff and also parents and carers whether they have a particular hobby or interest they would like to share, too.

Favourite food

Food preferences are one of the first ways we express our likes and dislikes. A young baby may screw up their face in disgust at one food, but may open their mouth wide and grab the spoon when offered another! By focusing on and sharing vocabulary that describes positive food experiences, children can not only learn from each other about the pleasure of a wide and varied diet but can also learn about differences in others' taste.

What you need:

▶ A variety of food items – include some more unusual fruits or vegetables

Preparation:

▶ With the children, discuss their favourite foods and ask questions such as:
  ▷ What words can you use to describe it?
  ▷ What colour is it?
  ▷ What texture is it?

What you do:

1. Show the children the food you have assembled, and see if any of them can name the more unusual items. Discuss the different colours, smells textures – and tastes!

2. Ask the children to create a simple riddle about their favourite food, including some of the adjectives they have been practising. The other children should try and guess the answers to the riddles.
   e.g.

   The food I like is crunchy,
   The food I like is hard,
   The food I like is orange.

   Can you guess?

   The food I like is carrots!

Key words:

smooth	crunchy	runny	sweet	salty	hot
cold	warm	wobbly			

Further fun:

▶ Suggest that the children have a role-play tea party. Ask them to use two words to describe each item of food that they are serving.

I love to wear...

Would you like to wear wellies all the time? Do you have a favourite hat that you take everywhere with you? Through our clothes choices we can express our mood, and our personality. Children love to express themselves creatively through their clothing choices and are often very attached to a particular item of clothing.

What you need:

▶ An assortment of clothes such as socks, t-shirts, dresses, jumpers, trousers coats, hats and gloves

▶ Large sheet of card

Preparation:

▶ Draw a child-sized outline on the sheet of card, and add features such as a face and hair.

▶ Discuss each item of clothing with the children:

▷ Why might we wear it?

▷ What is it made from?

▷ Why are different types of clothes made from different materials?

What you do:

1. Make the assortment of clothes available to the children and encourage them to explore the different types of clothing.

2. Ask the children to take it in turns to choose an item of clothing and place it on the drawn figure in the correct position.

3. Ask children to explain their choices: why did they put the article of clothing where they did? Discuss each choice as a group.

Key words:

soft   flowing   waterproof   warm   snuggly   bright

Further fun:

▶ Ask the children to bring in their own favourite clothes (with name tags on so items do not get misplaced) to dress the figure in.

This is me

It is important for young children to develop a sense of satisfaction in themselves and to recognise their own individuality. This activity encourages children to describe their appearances and understand that everyone is different.

What you need:

▶ Photographs of children in your class

▶ A4 paper

▶ Crayons or paints

Preparation:

▶ Encourage the children to talk about their own appearances. Ask:

▷ What colour is your hair?

▷ Is it straight or curly?

▷ What colour are your eyes?

What you do:

1. Show the children photographs of themselves.

2. Ask them to describe what they see.

3. Now, using the photographs for reference, ask each child to draw a self-portrait using crayons or paint.

> **Key words:**
>
> | | | | | | |
> |---|---|---|---|---|---|
> | blue | brown | green | sparkly | deep | curly |
> | straight | wavy | black | blonde | red | |

Further fun:

▶ Extend the activity by introducing similes. Ask the children to use similes to describe their eye colour. Are they blue like the sky or the sea? Are they brown like chocolate or autumn leaves?

Dressing up: people at work

The dressing up box provides endless opportunities for learning new words. Children can be doctors, nurses, firefighters, police officers, chefs... the list is endless. Each of these professions comes with its own vocabulary which is vital for children to understand and describe the world around them.

What you need:

▶ Dressing up uniforms

Preparation:

▶ Arrange the dressing up clothes so that they are clearly visible, and ask the children if they can name each one.

What you do:

1. Follow on by looking at the different features of each uniform and discuss why they look as they do. Ask questions such as:

   ▷ Why is it important that firefighters' uniforms can be easily seen?

   ▷ Why do you think some uniforms have pockets? What items might a doctor or nurse carry with them?

   ▷ Why do you think doctors often wear white coats?

2. Role-play 'hospitals'. As the children play, ask them about the equipment they are using and what illness they are treating.

Key words:

hospital	syringe	thermometer	bandage
plaster	medicine	poorly	stethoscope

Further fun:

▶ Create a scenario where different uniformed services have to come together to help someone. Ask for all children to offer suggestions as to what the story may be.

▶ Arrange for your local fire service to pay a visit. Discuss the equipment on the fire engine and the features of the firefighters' uniform.

Party clothes

Everyone loves a party, whether it be a large family gathering or a small get-together with a few close friends. But what to wear? This activity gives children the opportunity to explore vocabulary related to all that is smart and glamorous!

What you need:

▶ Dressing up party clothes

▶ Shiny and bright fabric scraps and collage materials

▶ Cut-out cardboard shapes of trousers, dresses and t-shirts

▶ Glue

Preparation:

Discussion:

▶ You are going to have a party. What will you wear? Discuss the children's choices.

▶ What colours does each child like to wear?

▶ In what way do party clothes differ from everyday clothes?

What you do:

1. Divide the children into groups of four, five or six, and offer each group a variety of dressing up clothes. Include party clothes such as hats and bow ties.

2. Provide each group with a cardboard cutout in the shape of an item of clothing.

3. Encourage the children to decorate the cardboard cutout using the collage material, so that it looks fabulous! Support their use of vocabulary as they are working, and test their knowledge by asking them questions about the materials they are working with.

Key words:

bows	smart	sparkle	glitter	clean
jacket	tie	best dress	ribbon	

Further fun:

▶ Have a class party! Get your favourite clothes on and get dancing.

▶ Ask the children to talk about their outfits using the vocabulary they have learned.

Dark and light

Dark and light, black and white: these pairings are the most basic descriptions of what we see around us. This activity encourages children to use vocabulary that moves beyond these simple opposites. 'Gloomy' or 'drab' can be used instead of 'dark', while 'light' can be replaced with 'bright' or 'dazzling'.

What you need:

▶ A dark place such as a tent or tunnel

▶ Torches

▶ Mirrors

▶ Reflective materials: foil strands and shapes, tinsel

Preparation:

▶ Discuss the key words on this page. Words such as 'drab' or 'shimmering' may be new to young children and are worth explaining and exploring.

What you do:

1. Ask the children to play in pairs inside the designated tent or dark place.

2. Provide each pair with a torch, and encourage them to illuminate particular areas inside the dark space. Suggest that they shine their torches on the reflective surfaces to see what happens.

3. After a session in the darkened area, discuss the differences between dark and light, and support the children in using the vocabulary from the 'key words' section.

Key words:

dark	dim	dull	drab	murky
light	gloomy	bright	shade	shadow
shine	dazzle	glitter	sparkling	shimmering

Further fun:

▶ Make a shadow play by hanging a white sheet from a washing line and darkening the room, then encouraging the children to stand between the sheet and the light, making shapes with their arms. Challenge them to create different shapes: can they make a shadow that looks like a bird? How about a shadow that looks like a tree?

The rainbow

Talking about the colours of the rainbow gives the opportunity to explore some common colour names, but also some that are less frequently used. Use this introduction to unusual colour words to explore even more: are there other words for different shades of 'red', for instance?

What you need:

▶ Scraps of tissue paper in rainbow colours

▶ White or coloured card

▶ Glue

Preparation:

▶ Look at and discuss pictures of rainbows.

▶ When do rainbows appear?

▶ Why do you think they appear?

▶ Discuss the different colours of the rainbow.

What you do:

1. Make rainbows to hang in your setting.

   ▷ Using sheets of card, cut out rainbow arc shapes.

   ▷ Draw six lines across each arc so that you have seven sections in total.

   ▷ Offer the children tissue paper in the seven colours of the rainbow.

   ▷ Remember: the colours of the rainbow always come in this order: red, orange, yellow, green, blue, indigo, violet.

   ▷ Challenge them to create their own rainbows by sticking the tissue paper pieces to the arc in the correct order!

Further fun:

▶ Look up the names of different artist's colours (acrylic paints have interesting names). Ask the children what colour they think each one might be: what shade is 'vermillion'? What about 'ultramarine'?

▶ Playing with purple: There are so many different shades of purple all with exciting names.

   ▷ Find pictures of objects that are different shades of purple. Discuss the names of the different shades. Can you see violet and indigo, lilac and mauve?

   ▷ Try mixing purple paint. Add white, red or blue to purple paint and talk about what happens to the colour.

▶ Have a 'rainbow clothing' day. Can you wear a piece of clothing that is one or more of the rainbow colours?

The rough and the smooth

Every object has texture, and there are lots of words to describe the way things feel. This activity gives children good practice in using adjectives to differentiate between items and teaches them to use language creatively.

What you need:

- Sandpaper
- Dough
- Plastic cup
- Twigs
- Silk fabric
- Toy hairbrush
- A pebble
- Wooden blocks, lego blocks or similar
- Cardboard box, shoebox, bag or similar

Preparation:

▶ Talk about the texture of the different objects you have collected.

▶ Introduce all the key words at the bottom of this page, ensuring that the children understand their meanings.

What you do:

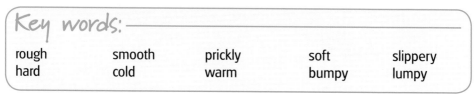

1. Place all the objects in the box.
2. The children take it in turns to pick an object from the box.
3. Can they describe the object while closing their eyes?
4. Challenge them to think of three words to describe the object they are holding.

Key words:

rough	smooth	prickly	soft	slippery
hard	cold	warm	bumpy	lumpy

Further fun:

▶ Can you find five smooth objects in your setting?

▶ Can you find five rough objects?

▶ What is the most interestingly textured object that you can find? Can you describe it?

Words for 'big'

'It's ginormous!', you may hear children say with great relish. 'It's humungous!' The joy with which young children adopt words to describe size can be used as a springboard to introduce some wonderful size-related vocabulary.

What you need:

Pictures of large objects such as:

▶ An elephant

▶ Big Ben

▶ A giraffe

▶ The sun

▶ A whale

Preparation:

▶ Discuss things that are large. How many things can you think of?

What you do:

1. Find as many pictures of 'big' things as you can. Find pictures on the internet or in magazines and cut them out.
2. Alternatively, encourage the children to draw their own pictures of animals or objects that they think are 'big'.
3. Create a 'big' wall display and add key words to the images.
4. Encourage the children to explore the display.

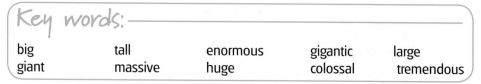

Key words:

big	tall	enormous	gigantic	large
giant	massive	huge	colossal	tremendous

Further fun:

▶ Go for a learning walk around your setting. How many huge, gigantic or enormous things can you see?

▶ Read stories containing enormous characters. Lots of fiction contains giants, elephants and, of course, enormous crocodiles!

Words for 'small'

Small things fascinate young children, who are often aware of their own physical size compared to the huge world around them. Tiny objects, whether small world sets or miniature versions of animals, are an important part of their play.

What you need:

A collection of miniature objects such as:

▶ Doll's house furniture

▶ Small world toys

▶ Small dolls' clothes

Preparation:

▶ Discuss the key words with the children and examine the small objects you have collected.

What you do:

1. Challenge the children to predict how many objects they can each fit in the palm of their hand.

2. Ask a child to choose four tiny items and see if they can hold them in one hand.

3. Now ask the child to say which objects they are holding, and to choose four 'small' words to describe the objects; for instance, 'a miniature horse', 'a little chair', 'a tiny person', 'a small shoe'.

> ### Key words:
>
> | small | tiny | miniature | little | mini |
> |---|---|---|---|---|
> | teeny | minute | microscopic | miniscule | |

Further fun:

▶ Plan a visit to a model village and play at being giants for a while!

Size similes

We often use similes when we talk about size. Similes compare two things using connecting words such as 'as', 'like', or 'though'. We often say 'as big as a' and 'as small as a', or 'smaller/bigger than a...'. Similes are important to vocabulary acquisition because they enable children to make connections between words.

What you need:

▶ Flashcards showing pictures of large objects
▶ Flashcards showing pictures of small objects

Preparation:

▶ Introduce the concept of similes.

▶ With the children, compare the small items using the flash cards, then compare the large items in the same way.

▶ Tell the story of *Jack and the Beanstalk*, drawing attention to the size vocabulary used.

What you do:

1. Discuss the large and small items in the story of *Jack and the Beanstalk*.

Large	Small
The beanstalk leaves	The beans
The beanstalk stem	Jack's house
The giant	Jack
The golden goose eggs	The harp

2. Can the children come up with similes for each item? For example: 'The golden egg was as big as a bed'!'

Key words: ────────────────────

as big as   as small as   smaller than   bigger than

Further fun:

Role-play being large and small:

I am a fairy and I am as tiny as...   a flower petal?
                                              a leaf
                                              a drop of rain?

I am a giant and I am as big as...   a house?
                                              an elephant?
                                              a yellow digger?

What other ideas can the children come up with?

Near and far

Positional language is essential if we are to describe the space around us and the location of objects within it. Positional vocabulary also allows us to articulate instructions and requests.

What you need:

▶ Toy blocks or bricks
▶ A small treasure chest to hide, filled with prizes of your choice

Preparation:

▶ Place two blocks on your lap and discuss positional vocabulary. Use the key words at the bottom of this page to describe the positions of the blocks.

▶ Give the children two blocks each and ask them to place them in a certain position, according to the key vocabulary you use.

What you do:

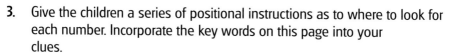

1. Hide a small treasure chest somewhere in your setting.

2. Hide laminated squares of paper around the setting, numbered 1-6.

3. Give the children a series of positional instructions as to where to look for each number. Incorporate the key words on this page into your clues.

4. Once they have found one number, read out the next clue using at least one key word so that they can find the next number.

5. Clue number six will lead them to the hidden treasure.

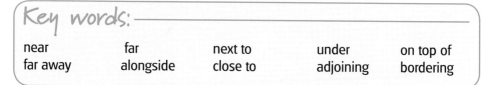

Key words:

near	far	next to	under	on top of
far away	alongside	close to	adjoining	bordering

Further fun:

▶ Create a map of your setting.

▶ Talk about which objects are next to each other.

▶ Which items are on top of something else?

Shapes

Words for shapes are not just important for developing mathematical awareness. Shapes also give us a descriptive vocabulary that allows us to talk about the world around us, from cars to castles!

What you need:

▶ Coloured card

▶ Scissors

Preparation:

▶ Using the card, cut out an assortment of shapes in varying sizes. Include squares, circles, diamonds, triangles and rectangles.

What you do:

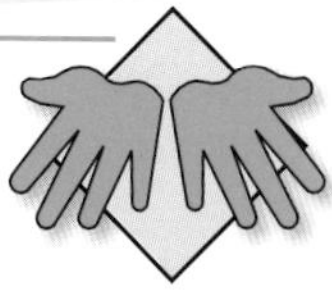

1. Show the children the different shapes, and talk about the name of each shape.

   ▷ Note the number of sides that each shape has.

   ▷ Discuss the fact that if something is triangle-shaped, we say it is triangular; if it is a circle we call it circular; a rectangle is rectangular, etc. Note that 'square' stays the same.

   ▷ Challenge the children to find shapes in your setting, e.g. "Who can see a circular object?"

2. Ask the children to make pictures using the card shapes.

3. Set them specific challenges: can you make a tree using rectangles and circles? Can you make a house using squares and triangles?

Key words:

square	triangle	triangular	circle	circular
circular	rectangular	diamond	diamond-shaped	

Further fun:

▶ Make an 'animal shape zoo', in which the children use card shapes to create interesting animals.

   ▷ Which shapes would you use to make a fish?

   ▷ Can you make a penguin?

Need for speed!

Children love to move their bodies in different ways, be it running, jumping, hopping or skipping. Play this fast-paced version of 'Mother, may I?' to explore nippy and zippy words!

What you need:

▶ A large space

▶ A whistle

Preparation:

▶ Talk about the key words at the bottom of this page.

What you do:

1. Ask the children to find a space.

2. Explain to the children that they will be moving about the space in different ways. Tell them that they have to shout 'Need for speed!' before they start moving, and that a blow of the whistle means that they need to stop.

3. Choose your instruction and deliver it to the children, making sure that it includes a key movement word. You might like to try:

▷ Run fast

▷ Jump nimbly

▷ Hop speedily

▷ Wave your arms rapidly

▷ Skip swiftly

Key words:

quickly	swiftly	fast	speedily	rapidly	nimbly

Further fun:

▶ Look at things that go fast and collect images of them for a 'speedy scrapbook'. Look for images of both animals and objects.

▶ Together, learn the rhyme below, 'Jack be Nimble':

Jack be nimble
Jack be quick
Jack jump over the candlestick!

Steady as a snail

Sometimes we need to stop rushing and just take things slowly. This activity prompts the use and exploration of vocabulary that tells us to slow down.

What you need:

▶ Plasticine or modelling clay

▶ A table

▶ Flowers and leaves cut out from sheets of card, in differing colours

Preparation:

▶ Look at pictures of snails and discuss the key vocabulary below.

▶ Ask questions such as:

▷ How do snails move?

▷ Why do you think they move so slowly?

▷ Have you ever found a snail in your garden?

▶ Lay the card, flowers and leaves around a table that is child height. Space them out so there is room between each flower and/or leaf.

What you do:

1. Support the children in making plasticine snails by rolling a strip of modeling clay between their palms then curling it up to make a snail shell. Add a second cylinder along the bottom to form the snail's body.

2. Ask each child to move their snail around the flower table according to your instructions, making sure that you choose a key word to describe each action. For instance:

▷ Can you 'dawdle' to a pink flower?

▷ Can you 'plod lazily' to a light green leaf?

> ### Key words:
>
> | slowly | plod | dawdle | steadily | sluggish |
> | unhurriedly | lazily | | | |

Further fun:

▶ Many slow and slimy words begin with the letter 's'! Challenge the children to try saying this snail tongue twister. They should start slowly and increase their speed as they become more confident:

The slow snail slips steadily,
The slimy snail sneaks slowly.

Speed similes

Similes and metaphors are perfect for describing speed and are commonly used by children. We all know what is implied if someone is described as 'a bit of a snail', or what it means to run 'as fast as a cheetah'. Because similes for speed are such a large part of our everyday vocabulary it is important that children clearly understand their meanings.

What you need:

▶ A large space!

Preparation:

▶ Discuss the following similes. Notice how many make comparisons to animals.

   ▷ As fast as lightning

   ▷ As quick as a wink

   ▷ As fast as a cheetah

   ▷ As steady as a snail

   ▷ As sluggish as a sloth

   ▷ As slow as an elephant

What you do:

1. Talk about the ways in which the children could act out each of the six speed similes you have just discussed. For instance, how might they move like a wink? (E.g. flash jazz hands; crouch down then leap up again...)

2. Divide the children into two groups: 'fast' and 'slow'.

3. Remind each group of their roles:

Fast	Slow
Lightning	A snail
A wink	A sloth
A cheetah	An elephant

4. Call out a speed simile and encourage the children to move around in that mode.

Key words:

fast	quick	sudden	jump	leap
flash	slow	crawl	slow motion	creep

Further fun:

▶ Can the children imagine and then draw the slowest creature in the world? What is its name and what does it look like? Can they do the same for the fastest creature in the world?

Moving on up: making a mountain

Encourage the children to use their imaginations as well as their vocabulary in this open-ended make-believe based activity.

What you need:

▶ Boxes and cushions

▶ Dolls or soft toys

Preparation:

▶ Discuss the key vocabulary at the bottom of this page.

▶ Model upward movements so that the children have a full understanding of the terms.

What you do:

1. Offer the children a variety of boxes and cushions, and challenge them to 'build a mountain'.

2. What special thing might be at the top of the mountain? Could it be:

    ▷ Treasure;

    ▷ A dragon;

    ▷ A friend;

    ▷ A castle?

3. Ask the children to move the toys up their mountain, encouraging them to use the key vocabulary as they do so.

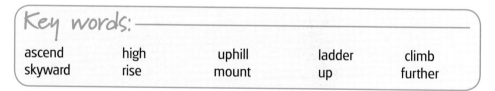

Key words:				
ascend	high	uphill	ladder	climb
skyward	rise	mount	up	further

Further fun:

▶ Use outdoor play equipment that children can climb.

▶ Support them in building tall towers with construction blocks and ask relevant questions using the key words as they build.

▶ If your setting and is in a hilly area, take a walk up a hill together. Ask questions to prompt the children's use of related vocabulary, such as: 'Are our legs getting tired?' and 'What do you think we'll see from the top?'

Moving down low: wiggly worms

Discover the world of wiggly worms and find out what can be seen at ground level!

What you need:

▶ An indoor space (with clean floors!)

▶ Cushions

Preparation:

▶ Discuss the key vocabulary on this page.

▶ Place cushions on the floor around your setting.

What you do:

1. Ask the children to lie on their tummies with their heads on the cushions.

2. Encourage them to describe what they can see when they are down low.

3. Make suggestions. Can they see:
   ▷ Chair legs
   ▷ Table legs
   ▷ Underneath cupboards?

4. Ask: 'What does the carpet look like when you are lying low on the ground like a worm?' 'What do shoes look like? Do they seem bigger?' 'What do the table legs look like?' Encourage the children to use similies they learned in 'Size similies' on page 51.

Key words:

| low | down | ground-level | bottom | shallow |
| beneath | | | | |

Further fun:

▶ If you have outdoor space and all-weather waterproof clothing, go outdoors and be wiggly worms outside! What does the outdoor world look like to a worm?

Twirling and whirling: spinning tops

This hands-on craft-based activity is a perfect way for children to explore the movement of spinning, twirling and whirling. How long can they keep their spinners spinning?

What you need:

▶ Circles of stiff card

▶ Crayons or felt-tip pens

▶ Sharpened pencils

▶ Sticky tack

Preparation:

▶ Collect and look at things that spin and twirl, such as video clips of:

▷ a washing machine

▷ spinning water whirling down a plughole

▷ roundabouts and play equipment

▷ aeroplane propellers

▷ helicopter blades

What you do:

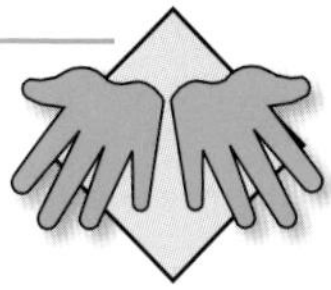

1. Give each child a circle of card and encourage them to draw whirly spiral patterns on the circle.

2. Help children to push a pencil through the centre of the circle.

3. Secure the pencil underneath the cardboard circle with a very small circle of sticky tack.

4. Challenge the children: "Can you make your spinners spin for five seconds without falling over?"

Key words:

| twirl | whirl | spin | twist | rotate | coil | curl |

Further fun:

▶ If you live near sycamore trees, in the autumn collect 'helicopter' seeds, take them outside, throw them in the air and watch them spin.

▶ Let the children dress up in twirly clothes. Can they make their cloaks and skirts whirl and swish?

▶ Make spiral mobiles and hang them in your setting.

Crouching, kneeling and bending

Words that describe low movements such as 'crouch' and 'hunch', 'dip' and 'duck' can be fun to say – and even more fun to enact! Turn part of your setting into a place that provides opportunities for these appealing new words to be used and explored.

What you need:

▶ Sheets

▶ Tables and chairs

▶ Washing line and pegs

Preparation:

▶ Create an environment where the children have to dip and duck, crouch and kneel to move around:

▷ Drape sheets over tables and chairs

▷ Hang and peg sheets from a washing line

What you do:

1. Discuss the key vocabulary and ask children to act out each word.

2. Now explore the transformed setting with the children.

3. Use words such as 'dip', 'crouch' and 'hunch' as you move through the space with them, and encourage them to describe their movements as they go.

Key words:

crouch	kneel	bend	hunch	dip
duck	crawl	bob	stoop	squat

Further fun:

▶ Which animals bob and dip? Watch video clips of bobbing and dipping birds, then re-enact the movements!

Slipping and sliding

So many slippery, slidey words begin with the 's' sound. Create a slithery wall display that explores words, objects and animals associated with this smooth letter.

What you need:

▶ Sugar paper
▶ Card
▶ Smooth and silky fabrics
▶ Pictures of slippery items: fish, snakes, jelly, soap...
▶ A display area

Preparation:

▶ Discuss the key words.

▶ Cut out large 's' shapes from the sugar paper and fix them so they are at child height in the display area.

What you do:

1. Look at the pictures of slippery items and handle some smooth and silky fabrics.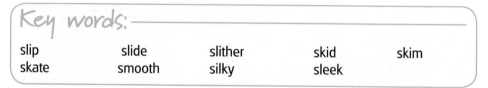

2. Ask the children: "What does the silky material feel like?"

3. Choose smooth and silky fabrics and attach these to your letter 's' display.

4. Let the children add pictures to the display, and encourage them to describe each object or item as they attach the picture to the display.

Key words:

slip	slide	slither	skid	skim
skate	smooth	silky	sleek	

Further fun:

▶ Play on slides and explore frictionless, smooth surfaces.

▶ Can the children write a sentence using three or more 's' words?

The noisy dinosaur

Warning: this rhyme is noisy! Making a loud noise can be very enjoyable, but it is important that children learn to stop when you raise your hand during this activity. Some children find loud noises unsettling, so use your professional judgement when determining the appropriate timing and location for this activity.

What you need:

▶ A range of percussion instruments

Preparation:

▶ Practise making a loud sound and then stopping:

▷ Ask the children to 'roar like a dinosaur'.

▷ Ask them to stop as soon as you hold up your hand.

▷ Practise this execise until all children learn to stop!

What you do:

1. Learn the rhyme:

Roar roar roar like a dinosaur (*roar three times*)

Bang bang bang on the drum (*bang three times*)

Crash crash crash through the tall, tall trees (*stamp feet*)

Our fun has just begun!

Shout shout shout like you want some more (*shout three times*)

Bang bang bang on the drum

Crash crash crash through the tall tall trees

And now our noise is done.

2. Try using an assortment of percussion instruments to accompany the rhyme and really make a noise!

> Key words:
>
> noisy   loud   shout   bang   crash   roar

Further fun:

▶ Make a variety of instruments out of junk to create a noisy junk orchestra.

▶ Invite a percussion group to give a performance in your setting.

In the whispering grass

Sounds can be quiet and gentle as well as noisy and loud. Create an imaginative soundscape using junk materials and your voices to explore words that do things nice and quietly. Shhhh!

What you need:

▶ Pebbles or sand
▶ Empty yoghurt pots
▶ Muslin squares
▶ Elastic bands

Preparation:

▶ Fill the bottom of the yoghurt pots with pebbles or sand.

▶ Cover the tops of the pots with a square of muslin and secure with an elastic band.

What you do:

1. Divide the children into four groups:

   Group 1: Sand pot shakers

   Group 2: Whisperers

   Group 3: Mutterers

   Group 4: Sighers

2. Ask each group to practise making their sounds.

3. Now make your soundscape. Describe the following scene in a very quiet voice and ask the children to imagine they are there:

   We are in a field on a warm still day.

   The grass is murmurming *(murmurers)*

   The leaves are whispering and sighing *(whisperers and sighers)*

   A stream runs nearby *(sand pot shakers)*

   And it flows gently over some rocks.

4. Now repeat the story, encouraging the relevant groups to move as you feel it.

5. Ask the children: 'Can you make the whispering grass soundscape with your eyes closed? What do you imagine the scene looks like?'

> ## Key words:
>
> whisper   mutter   hush   murmur   sigh
> mumble

Further fun:

▶ Play a classic game of Chinese Whispers.

   ▷ The children sit in a circle and one child begins the game by whispering a silly sentence to the child sitting to his or her left.

   ▷ Remembering to whisper, each child in turn passes the sentence on to the person on their left, until the sentence has been passed around the whole group.

   ▷ Is the sentence you finish with the same as the one you started with?

Why does the duck say 'quack'?

There are many books, songs, games and activities that explore the sounds that animals make. Children often become familiar with vocabulary that describes animal noises before they learn to describe the many ways in which people speak. This activity uses this familiarity to encourage children to explore and articulate their ideas and opinions.

What you need:

▶ Pictures of a:
  ▷ Duck
  ▷ Cow
  ▷ Horse
  ▷ Bird
  ▷ Snake
  ▷ Frog

Preparation:

▶ Show the children the animal pictures and discuss the sounds that each animal makes.

▶ As a group, practise making the sounds yourselves!

What you do:

1. Now hold up and introduce each animal picture with the words: "Once upon a time there was a duck who suddenly gave a loud quack!"

2. Ask for ideas as to why he might have quacked.

3. Repeat this process for each animal.

> ### Key words:
>
> quack   moo   neigh   cheep   hiss   croak

Further fun:

▶ Play the soft toy 'sounds' game.

  ▷ Seat the children in a circle.

  ▷ Place a variety of small beanie-type animal toys in a bag on your lap.

  ▷ Draw out one toy and gently throw it to a child, asking them to make the sound the animal makes.

  ▷ Enrich their vocabulary by describing the way in which the toy sounds: "Can you make the dog bark sadly?'; 'Can you make the lion roar gently?"; "Can you make the snake hiss ferociously?"

Words for speaking

We use our voices in so many different ways. The words we use to describe the way we speak show us not only what we are trying to communicate but also how we are communicating it. Understanding why people speak in different ways, tones and volumes improves children's empathy and social skills.

What you need:

▶ Your voices!

Preparation:

▶ As a group, practise whispering, shouting, murmuring and declaring. 'Whispering' and 'shouting' are common words that the children are likely to understand. 'Murmuring' and 'declaring' are words that may have to be explored together and experienced in more detail.

What you do:

1. Use the sentence 'I don't want to go to the park' to explore a variety of ways of speaking. Ask the children to:

   ▷ Whisper it

   ▷ Shout it

   ▷ Murmur it

   ▷ Declare it

2. Now explore the possible intentions behind these choices. Why might someone whisper the sentence? Why might they shout it? Why might they murmur it? Why might they declare it?

> ## Key words:
>
> whisper   shout   murmur   declare   cry   yell
> say   reply

Further fun:

▶ During story time, highlight and focus on words that mean 'said'.

▶ Ask: "Why do you think the author uses different words?"

▶ How many different words for 'said' can the children collect?

Vehicles

Our everyday world when out and about is full of noise, much of which is made by vehicles. From beeping car horns and slamming doors to the high-above drone of a passing airplane, we can explore lots of noisy transport words.

What you need:

▶ Toy or small world cars, lorries and buses

▶ Ride-on toys

Preparation:

▶ Discuss different vehicle noises as the children play with small world vehicles or ride-on toys.

▶ Ask the children what sounds a car, bus, train, plane and helicopter each make.

What you do:

1. Tell the children to imagine that they are going to go on a car journey to the seaside.

2. Ask them to make sounds for each part of the journey. Ideas might include the following:

   ▷ Open the car door: creak

   ▷ Shut the car door: slam

   ▷ Turn on the engine: chug, chug, chug

   ▷ Off you go: vroom!

   ▷ There's a sheep in the road!: beep beeeeep!

   ▷ You're nearly there so put the breaks on: squeak

   ▷ Open the car door: creak

   ▷ Shut the car door: slam

3. Expand on your vehicle sound-story using suggestions from the children. What other vehicles might you see on your journey? What sounds might they make?

Key words:

creak	slam	chug	vroom	beep	honk
squeak	whirr	zoom			

Further fun:

▶ Be sound detectives and collect some vehicle sounds.

   ▷ Stand outside and listen. Support the children in noting down and/or recording any vehicle sounds that they hear.

Kitchen orchestra

Our houses are never quiet, even if we try to be! In the bathroom, toilets flush and taps drip. In bedrooms and sitting rooms, cupboards and drawers creak and slam and hoovers drone. But it's the kitchen where things really get noisy: microwaves ping, the dishwasher sloshes, vegetables are chopped and kettles boil.

What you need:

▶ A home kitchen area, fully resourced

Preparation:

▶ Discuss things that happen in the kitchen. What kinds of sounds are made by the different activities?

What you do:

1. Make a pretend meal in your home kitchen. Focus on the sounds that the actions make.
2. Ask the children to narrate their play, focusing on sound words – see key words on this page for ideas.
3. Make a note of the actions carried out and the vocabulary used.
4. Now perform this rhyme with full orchestration!

    It's kitchen music time,
    It's time to sweep and rhyme
    Brush the floor, swish swish
    Mop some more, slosh slosh
    Wash the dishes, splosh splosh
    Plates away, clatter clatter
    Now forks and spoons, jingle jangle
    Wring the cloth, twist and mangle:
    Ok, are we done?
    No, we've just begun! (*Repeat rhyme.*)

Key words:

ping	splash	scrape	clatter	swoosh	ding
brush	clang				

Further fun:

▶ Carry out a sitting room survey. Ask children, with the help of parents and carers, to find four noises that happened in the sitting room before bedtime. The television only counts as one noise!

▶ Together, explore vocabulary that describes the different sounds. Did the TV chatter? The sofa scrunch? Did the radiators gurgle? Did people talk or pets miaow or bark?

Sloshing and washing

Water is fun to play with and gives us lots of 'splosh' and 'drip' words. It 'pours' or 'drizzles' from the sky, 'swishes' around our mouth as we brush our teeth and 'gurgles' as it goes down the plughole. Many water words are onomatopoeic: they make the sound that they describe.

What you need:

- ▶ A water play area, outdoors or indoors
- ▶ Watering can
- ▶ Jug
- ▶ Cups and beakers

Preparation:

▶ Discuss the vocabulary in the key words box.

▶ Look at the different ways we use water. For example:

▷ We drink it

▷ We wash with it

▷ We swim and play in it

What you do:

1. Using the water area and water toys, ask children to choose a toy that will make water do the following:

▷ Pour

▷ Drip

▷ Trickle

▷ Dribble

▷ Flow

2. Talk to each child about what the water is doing. Prompt them to use watery vocabulary as they describe their actions to you.

> ### Key words:
>
> | | | | | |
> |---|---|---|---|---|
> | pour | drip | splash | trickle | dribble |
> | stream | flow | | | |

Further fun:

▶ If you have wellies and waterproofs available, take the children to splash in puddles on a rainy day. Talk about what you are doing with the water.

Water safety: remind children that although water is lots of fun, they should never play with water without an adult nearby.

The **Little Books** series consists of:

50
All through the year
Bags, Boxes & Trays
Big Projects
Bricks & Boxes
Celebrations
Christmas
Circle Time
Clay and Malleable Materials
Clothes and Fabric
Colour, Shape and Number
Cooking from Stories
Cooking Together
Counting
Dance
Dens
Discovery Bottles
Dough
Drama from Stories
Explorations
Fine Motor Skills
Free and Found
Fun on a Shoestring
Games with Sounds
Gross Motor Skills
Growing Things
Investigations
Junk Music
Kitchen Stuff
Language Fun
Light and Shadow

Listening
Living Things
Look and Listen
Making Books and Cards
Making Poetry
Maps and Plans
Mark Making
Maths Activities
Maths from Stories
Maths Outdoors
Maths Problem Solving
Maths Songs and Games
Messy Play
Minibeast Hotels
Multi-sensory Stories
Music
Music and Movement
Numbers
Nursery Rhymes
Opposites
Outdoor Play
Outside in All Weathers
Painting
Parachute Play
Persona Dolls
Phonics
Playground Games
Print Making
Prop Boxes for Role Play
Props for Writing
Puppet Making

Puppets in Stories
Resistant Materials
Rhythm and Raps
Role Play
Role Play Windows
Sand and Water
Science through Art
Scissor Skills
Seasons
Sequencing Skills
Sewing and Weaving
Shape and Space
Small World Play
Sound Ideas
Special Days
Stories from around the world
Story bags
Storyboards
Storybuilding
Storytelling
Time and Money
Time and Place
Topsy Turvy
Traditional Tales
Treasure Baskets
Treasure Boxes
Tuff Spot Activities
Washing lines
Woodwork
Writing

All available from
www.bloomsbury.com/featherstone

The Little Books Club

There is always something in Little Books to help and inspire you. Packed full of lovely ideas, Little Books meet the need for exciting and practical activities that are fun to do, address the Early Learning Goals and can be followed in most settings. Everyone is a winner!

We publish 5 new Little Books a year. Little Books Club members receive each of these 5 books as soon as they are published for a reduced price. The subscription cost is £29.99 – a one off payment that buys the 5 new books for £4.99 instead of £8.99 each.

In addition to this, Little Books Club Members receive:
· Free postage and packing on anything ordered from the Featherstone catalogue
· A 15% discount voucher upon joining which can be used to buy any number of books from the Featherstone catalogue
· Members price of £4.99 on any additional Little Book purchased
· A regular, free newsletter dealing with club news, special offers and aspects of Early Years curriculum and practice
· All new Little Books on approval - return in good condition within 30 days and we'll refund the cost to your club account

Call 020 7458 0200 or email: littlebooks@bloomsbury.com for an enrolment pack. Or download an application form from our website:
www.bloomsbury.com